U.S. Inequality & Economic Growth

A Call for a Deeper Dive

By Michael D. Williams

Copyright © 2018 by Michael D. Williams

All rights reserved. No part of this book may be used or reproduced in any manner whatsoever, including Internet usage, without the written permission of the author.

Cover design by Michael D. Williams

Contents

Executive Summary	05
Inequality Metrics	11
Gross Domestic Product [GDP]	15
Inequality, GDP and GDP Growth	23
What's Behind the Inverse Relationship?	27
Conclusions	31
Appendix A: Statistical Appendix	35
Gross Domestic Product	
Inequality Metrics	
Appendix B: Bibliography	47
Acknowledgements	57

Executive Summary

Income inequality has been worsening in the U.S. during the last few decades. As it worsens, a larger portion of U.S. income goes to those in the top income brackets, which means those below the top get a smaller and smaller share. There are several reasons this is not good for the U.S. and the reasons are what motivated me to write this eStudy. The reasons increased income inequality is not good for the U.S. are the following:

- Higher income **inequality** portends more poverty, a sicker population, and a shrinking middle class. All of these hinder U.S. economic growth and prosperity.
- Greater income **inequality** provides the wealthy young with greater opportunity than the poor young. If we want the poor to have a better chance to succeed – and provide benefits to the rest of the country – then improved income equality is a must.
- Greater income **inequality** provides the wealthy with greater influence on the political process. A corollary implication is that the wealthy have greater influence over the lives of those less well off.

Greater income inequality is a burden on society. For the less well-off there are issues with health, education or skills, earning a basic living, and saving for retirement.

6 | Executive Summary

This eStudy attempts to explain the link between income inequality and economic growth and does so using an economic microscope. When economic growth is slower in the U.S., companies do not make as many domestic investments, hire as many people or take other steps to expand their production.

Inequality can be defined in a number of ways. For this eStudy, the main focus is inequality of income and the country examined is the United States. The primary metrics used to represent Income Inequality are the Gini coefficient, and the share of total income associated with the Top 1% of all wage earners. The Gini coefficient – developed by the Italian statistician Corrado Gini in 1912 – is a measure of the dispersion of income in a country. A score of zero means there is complete equality of income. A score of 1.0 means all the income is attributed to one person. The data for this analysis runs from 1944 through 2016 and is in Appendix A.

The inequality metrics are compared to U.S. Gross Domestic Product [GDP] in constant 2009 $ to ascertain their relationship. It is not unusual to posit that GDP and inequality move together, yielding no reason to be concerned with the level of inequality. Plotting U.S. GDP with the U.S. Gini coefficient reveals a strong positive linear relationship for the period 1944 through 2016. On the surface this seems to allay fears that the economy might be impacted by inequality. But the reality is different ... as inequality increases, the *rate* of economic growth decreases.

Initial analysis used annual data but it was difficult to ascertain trends due to business cycles. The analysis was switched to a 5-year moving average of the data and it was learned there is a moderately weak inverse relationship between inequality and GDP growth, that is to say, greater income inequality is associated with slower economic growth.

To understand the reason for this relationship, one needs to look no further than the components of GDP. The reason the Gini – GDP growth correlation – is not stronger, is that other components of GDP can dominate and lead the economy. For example, between 1951 and 1969, government expenditures grew an average of 8.9% per year in nominal terms and averaged 23.1% of GDP – three points higher than the average for 1970 to 2016 when government expenditures averaged 20.1% of GDP. Also during 1951-1969, there was a trade surplus as Net Exports grew at an average of 60.5% per year and averaged +0.5% of GDP. By contrast, the U.S. ran a trade deficit that averaged -2.1% of GDP between 1970 and 2016 as Net Exports contracted 25% per year. Thus, exports became a drag on the economy after 1970 at the same time government's share in the economy was declining and its growth rate fell to 5.8% per year in nominal terms. Private sector investment has been fairly stable over time – averaging 16.4% of GDP between 1951 and 1969 and 17.6% for the period 1970 to 2016. Personal consumption increased from 60.1% of GDP between 1951 and 1969 to 64.4% of GDP from 1970 to 2016 and has the fastest growth rate of the four components during the 1970 to 2016 time frame. Thus, it appears consumption is the new economic leader. So what is the rub?

As inequality increases, a larger portion of the income goes to a smaller share of the population and those with the larger incomes tend to save more than those with lower incomes. The combined effect on the economy from all the households – a larger share of aggregate savings and a smaller share of aggregate consumption – leads to slower economic growth. With slower economic growth, there is less demand for goods and services and companies don't need to make additional investments. As a sidelight, with slower economic growth there is less tax revenue to fund the government.

So it makes sense that the correlation between inequality and economic growth is not stronger because other components of GDP have lead the economy during different periods between 1951 and 2016. Since 1985 – after consumption became the leader – the correlation between Gini and GDP growth strengthened.

A word to the wise, more research needs to be done on this topic. This is initial analysis using basic data in an effort to understand cause and effect. While I strongly believe that increased inequality leads to slower economic growth, others need to undertake in-depth analysis and see what they learn. In its research, the International Monetary Fund [IMF] found that countries with greater income equality had longer expansion phases and shallower recessions. However, a recent blog on the IMF website points to inconclusive results regarding the results of inequality's impact on economic development

If my thesis holds [greater inequality implies slower economic growth], then there are policy implications for improving economic growth in the U.S. Policies that improve health and education can improve the productivity of the U.S. workers, decrease income inequality and accelerate U.S. economic growth. And these expenditures can be funded by a more progressive income tax system that further reduces income inequality.

10 | Executive Summary

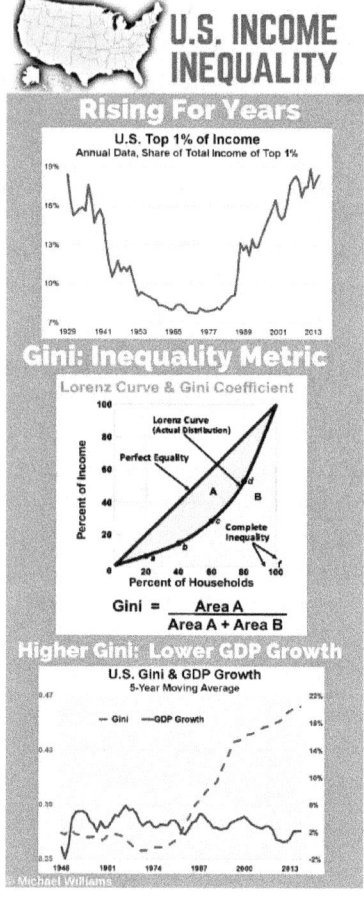

Inequality Metrics

The inequality metrics obtained for this eStudy are the following:

- Gini Coefficient
- Top 1% Income
- Top 1% Net Wealth

Analysis is done with the income metrics using annual data and 5-year moving average data. Shown below are the three sets of inequality metrics plotted for the time period 1944 to 2016.

Several observations when looking at this data:

- The general trend for all three indicators is flat to slightly decreasing until about 1980.
- All three of the indicators tend to increase after 1985 – but they all increase at different rates – this is important and will be used later in the analysis.
- The Gini coefficient has a narrower range varying from about 0.351 in 1968 to 0.464 in 2016. This is a range of about 32% of the low value. By contrast, the Top 1% of Income has a range of about 144% of the low value [7.7% in 1973 and 18.9% in 2012]. The Top 1% of Net Wealth falls somewhere in between with a range of about 80% of the low value. Thus, the Gini tends to be more stable while the Top 1% of income is the most volatile.
- The correlation between the Gini coefficient and the Top 1% Income is +0.942. This makes sense since the Top 1% of income is a factor in computing Gini.
- The correlation between the Gini coefficient and the Top 1% of Net Wealth is +0.727. This correlation is much weaker than the correlation between Gini and Income and makes sense as Net Wealth may not be a function of current income.

To better view the long-term trends, the 5-year moving average is estimated for each of the inequality indicators and plotted below.

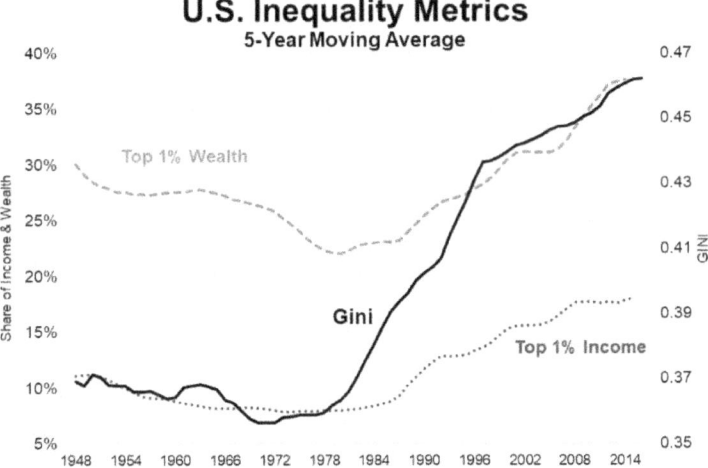

Using the 5-year moving average removes the annual volatility and makes the trends more prominent.

14 | Inequality Metrics

Gross Domestic Product [GDP]

The Gross Domestic Product [GDP] data used in this eStudy are the following:

- GDP in constant 2009 U.S. Dollars [US$]
- GDP components to include: Personal Consumption, Gross Private Domestic Investment, Government Consumption and Investment Expenditures and Net Exports of Goods and Services

Analysis of the GDP date includes computing the following:

- Annual rates of change
- 5-year moving average rate of change
- The shares of the GDP components
- The annual changes in each of the GDP components

A simple chart is created to show GDP in constant 2009$ for the period 1944 to 2016.

16 | Gross Domestic Product [GDP]

For the entire period, it appears GDP in constant 2009 US$ grew at a very even pace with only a few ups and downs – and it averaged 2.9% per year. However, this hides real variation due to business cycles and recessions. To get a sense of the volatility, annual changes are estimated for each year of the period and plotted on the following chart.

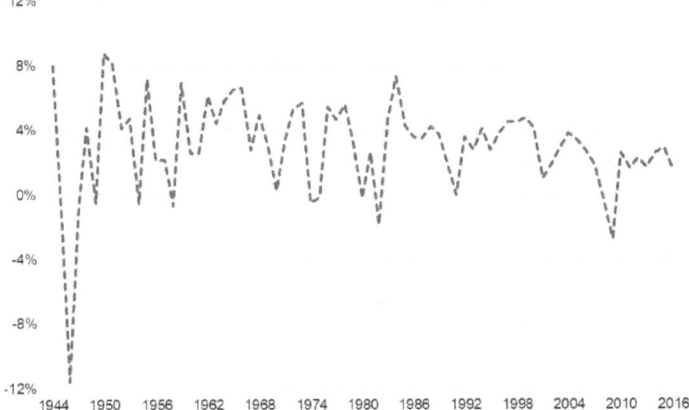

Now you can see the volatility. While GDP growth averaged 2.9% per year, the maximum one-year contraction was -11.6% in 1946, while the largest one-year gain was 8.7% in 1950. This leads to an interesting finding: the size of the variations has decreased over time. From 1951 to 1969 the average annual change was 4.2%. Between 1970 and 2016, the average annual change was 2.8%. Thus, the average volatility of **annual changes** in GDP in constant 2009 US$ **decreased 33%.**

Many factors are at work in the U.S. economy, including the smooth operations of the U.S. Federal Reserve. But there appears to be some sort of structural change occurring. To get a better sense of the trend, the 5-year moving average of annual changes in GDP is plotted.

5-Year Moving Average of Annual % Changes

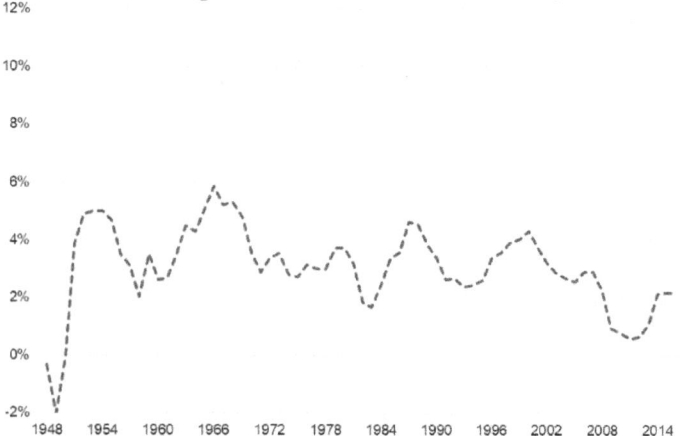

The decrease in volatility is more prominent using the 5-year moving average data. In fact, this decrease in volatility was discovered by visually examining the moving 5-year average of GDP changes and formed the basis for using the two major time periods of 1951 to 1969 and 1970 to 2016 for this eStudy.

We know that business cycles and recessions cause downturns, but how have the different components of

GDP acted during this period? For this analysis we begin in 1951 – after the war.

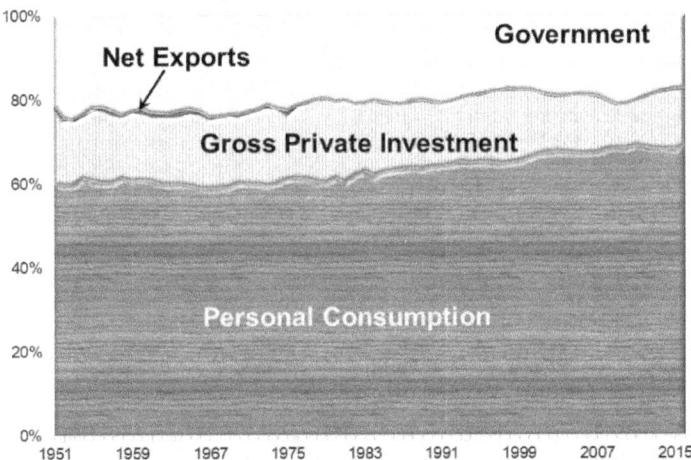

Components of U.S. GDP

Over the period 1951 to 2016, the share of U.S. GDP accounted for by personal consumption has averaged about 63.2%; Gross Private Investment has averaged 17.2%. Government [both consumption and investment] has averaged 21.0% and Net Exports have averaged -1.4% of GDP per year. These overall averages hide changes that have occurred over time.

Gross Domestic Product [GDP]

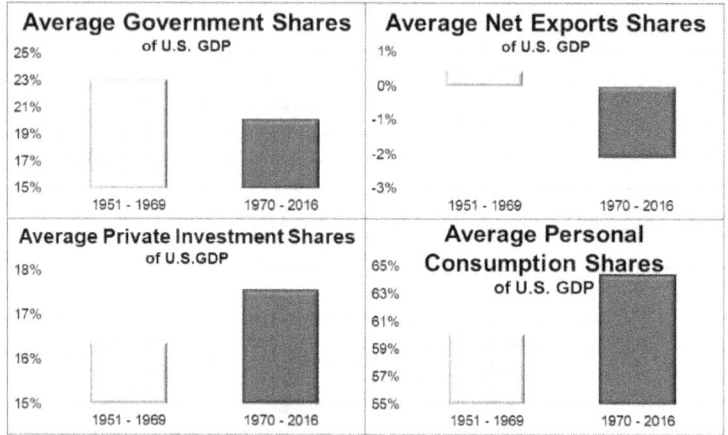

As different parts of the economy expand, it causes GDP to expand. Over time, different parts of the economy have been the leader in this expansion. By examining sector shares and sector growth rates, one can observe the relationship between the two.

Between 1951 and 1969, the government sector was the leader as government expenditures averaged 23.1% of GDP – three points higher than the average for 1970 to 2016 when government expenditures averaged 20.1% of GDP. Nominal growth in government expenditures averaged 8.9% growth during this period – the fastest of any sector – see chart below.

Also during the period 1951 to 1969, there was a trade surplus that averaged +0.5% of GDP per year as nominal net exports grew at an average of 60.5% per year. By contrast, the U.S. ran a trade deficit that averaged -2.1% of GDP between 1970 and 2016 and nominal net exports contracted at an annual rate of 25.6% per year. Thus, exports became a drag on the economy after 1970 at the same time government's share in the economy was declining.

Private sector investment has been volatile when you look at individual years, but over time the averages are similar. Between 1951 and 1969 private sector investment averaged 16.4% of GDP. For the period 1970 to 2016, the average is slightly higher at 17.6%.

Personal consumption increased from 60.1% of GDP between 1951 and 1969 to 64.4% of GDP from 1970 to 2016. In nominal terms, personal consumption grew 6.8% per year for the period 1970 to 2016, faster than the other sectors [see chart below]. Since personal consumption is driving more of GDP growth, changes in personal income would be expected to have an effect on consumption, and thus on growth. So it appears consumption is the new economic leader.

The period 1985 to 2016 is included in the analysis because **all** of the inequality metrics are increasing after 1985 – see the Inequality Metrics, 5-Year Moving Average chart.

22 | Gross Domestic Product [GDP]

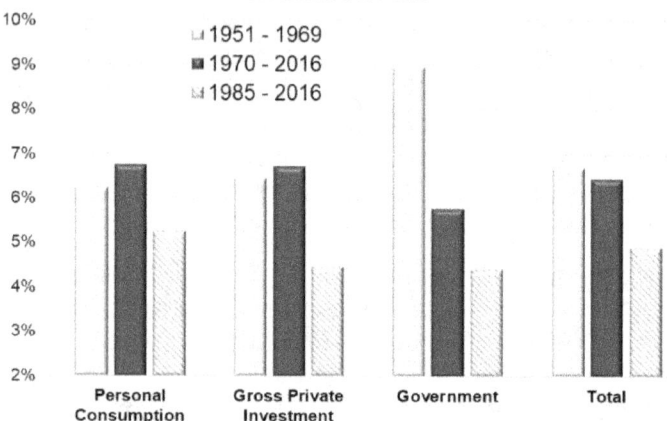

Inequality, GDP and GDP Growth

We begin this section by plotting the Gini coefficient with U.S. GDP in constant 2009 US$. The correlation between the two series is +0.944. See chart below.

It is the high correlation that prompts many to think there is no negative influence of inequality on the U.S. economy. But the effect is present in the second order, that is, the effect of income inequality on economic growth. To highlight this trend, the 5-year moving average of GDP growth is plotted with the 5-year moving average of the Gini coefficient and the Top 1% of Income holders.

The correlation between the Gini coefficient and U.S. economic growth is -0.354 for the period 1948 to 2016 using the 5-year moving average data. The correlation is lower for the Top 1% at -0.287.

As was noted in the GDP section, annual volatility decreased about 33% after 1970 and inequality increased substantially after 1980 – with all of the inequality metrics increasing after 1985. Since we are now using the 5-year moving average data, the correlation for the Gini coefficient and U.S. economic growth is estimated for the period 1985 to 2016 and is -0.581 – substantially larger than that for the entire period. It is also after 1985 that we see economic growth grind lower to an average of 2.6% per year.

Inequality, GDP and GDP Growth

What's Behind the Inverse Relationship?

The U.S. economy is driven by consumption and since 1970 about 64% of the U.S. economy is personal consumption. Gross private investment represents about 17½%, government represents about 20% and net exports represents about -2%. Also, of the four GDP components, personal consumption has the fastest growth rate averaging 6.8% per year in nominal terms for the period 1970 to 2016.

People spend and save based on their level of income. Those with very low levels of income consume virtually all their income and may borrow to supplement their income. Individuals in the Top 1% have such large incomes they save more than 50% of their income. This information was published by the Journal of Political Economy in 2004.

28 | What's Behind the Inverse Relationship?

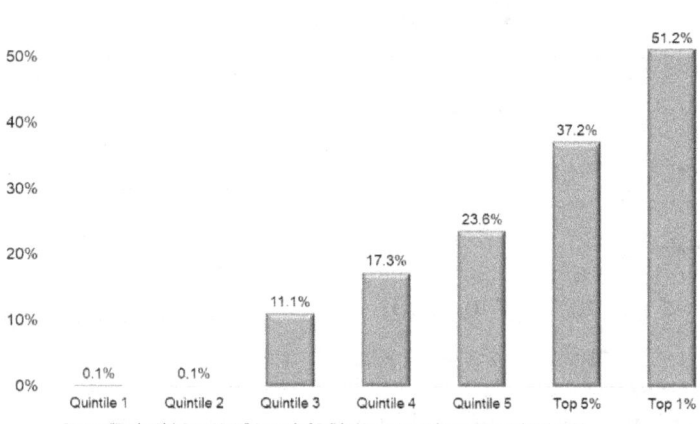

Source: "Do the Rich Save More", Journal of Political Economy, Volume 112, number 2, 2004

It is this disparity in the consumption and saving rates that leads to the conclusion that increased income inequality is associated with slower economic growth.

The reason the correlation is not stronger, is because different sectors of the economy took leadership during different periods of time and spurred economic growth. Everything in the economy is related – directly or indirectly – to everything else. For example, high oil prices might stimulate a company to invest in oil development, which can lead to hiring and expansion, which may influence income inequality. This is a complex topic and trying to parse out the effect of income inequality is challenging. As outlined in the GDP section, the government sector and net exports led through 1969. Gross private investment has been fairly constant during the entire time frame used in this study. Since 1970 personal consumption has averaged about 64% of U.S. GDP and since 1980 the rate of inequality has been growing. Thus, it is in the last 30 years that personal consumption is in the leadership role and inequality is widening.

30 | What's Behind the Inverse Relationship?

Conclusions

For those who still don't believe income inequality affects economic growth, consider the decade 1950 to 1959. What you learn from the data is that GDP growth averaged +4.3% per year while income inequality declined an average of 0.1% per year. During this decade the marginal tax rate for the Top 1% was greater than 90%, federal government expenditures were growing rapidly as the government had programs for GIs returning from war that allowed them to purchase homes and obtain education. Also, social security had begun payments to the elderly. All of these programs helped low and middle-income individuals, reducing income inequality. The policies after World War II spurred equality and economic growth.

Comparing U.S. Gini and U.S. GDP Average Annual Growth Rates For Two Different Decades

	1950 - 1959	2000 - 2009
GDP Growth in 2009 US$	+4.3%	+1.8%
Gini Coefficient	-0.1%	+0.3%

Comparing the GDP growth and Gini from the 1950s to the decade that ran from 2000 to 2009 reveals a

Conclusions

different economic environment. During the more recent decade, GDP growth averaged +1.8% per year [a decrease of 58% from the 1950s decade] and the Gini was increasing +0.3%. During this decade, government expenditures declined as a sequester was put in place. The great recession of 2008 occurred and its impact was felt by everyone – including the wealthy who saw their wealth and income decline substantially – which caused income inequality to lessen. As the economy and the stock market recovered, the wealthy recovered disproportionately more than middle and low-income households, which meant inequality increased and more than offset the initial decline in 2007. Finally, the marginal tax rate for the Top 1% varied between 35% and 39.1% depending on the year selected. Note: in no year since 2000 has economic growth been as high as the average for the 1950s.

This analysis has scratched the surface of understanding the relationship between income inequality and economic growth. I used basic GDP data and its components to portray the U.S. economy. I used basic analysis – growth rates, and shares of GDP to paint a picture of the manner in which the U.S. economy has functioned.

For the inequality metrics, I used data already compiled and spliced three series together to create a long time series of inequality. Using the 5-year moving average

Conclusions | 33

was helpful as it made it easier to see the trends without the noise of the business cycles. Future research might compute original Gini coefficients and go all the way back to the beginning of federal income taxes. This would be before the stock market crash of 1929, and might shed light on inequality and economic growth in an earlier era.

If more research comes to the same conclusion reached here, then more robust economic growth can be facilitated by greater income equality. While this is not the only factor influencing the growth of the U.S. economy, it would provide clear guidance on policy choices that impact equality and economic growth. I want to believe there is an inverse relationship between inequality and economic growth, but it would be great if others would add to this research to expand knowledge in this area and substantiate my claim.

34 | Conclusions

Appendix A: Statistical Appendix

There are two major categories of U.S. data:

- Gross Domestic Product [GDP] and the components of GDP
- Inequality Metrics – Gini Coefficient, Top 1% Share of Income, Top 1% of Net Wealth

Gross Domestic Product [GDP]

All the GDP data come from the U.S. Bureau of Economic Analysis. For this work, GDP is in Constant 2009 US$.

US Economic Indicator, Gross Domestic Product [GDP]

	GDP in constant 2009 US$	Changes in GDP Annual	Changes in GDP 5-Year Moving Average		GDP in constant 2009 US$	Changes in GDP Annual	Changes in GDP 5-Year Moving Average
1944	2,239.4	8.0%		1981	6,617.7	2.6%	3.1%
1945	2,217.8	-1.0%		1982	6,491.3	-1.9%	1.8%
1946	1,960.9	-11.6%		1983	6,792.0	4.6%	1.6%
1947	1,939.4	-1.1%		1984	7,285.0	7.3%	2.5%
1948	2,020.0	4.2%	-0.3%	1985	7,593.8	4.2%	3.4%
1949	2,008.9	-0.5%	-2.0%	1986	7,860.5	3.5%	3.5%
1950	2,184.0	8.7%	-0.1%	1987	8,132.6	3.5%	4.6%
1951	2,360.0	8.1%	3.9%	1988	8,474.5	4.2%	4.5%
1952	2,456.1	4.1%	4.9%	1989	8,786.4	3.7%	3.8%
1953	2,571.4	4.7%	5.0%	1990	8,955.0	1.9%	3.4%
1954	2,556.9	-0.6%	5.0%	1991	8,948.4	-0.1%	2.6%
1955	2,739.0	7.1%	4.7%	1992	9,266.6	3.6%	2.7%
1956	2,797.4	2.1%	3.5%	1993	9,521.0	2.7%	2.4%
1957	2,856.3	2.1%	3.1%	1994	9,905.4	4.0%	2.4%
1958	2,835.3	-0.7%	2.0%	1995	10,174.8	2.7%	2.6%
1959	3,031.0	6.9%	3.5%	1996	10,561.0	3.8%	3.4%
1960	3,108.7	2.6%	2.6%	1997	11,034.9	4.5%	3.6%
1961	3,188.1	2.6%	2.7%	1998	11,525.9	4.4%	3.9%
1962	3,383.1	6.1%	3.5%	1999	12,065.9	4.7%	4.0%
1963	3,530.4	4.4%	4.5%	2000	12,559.7	4.1%	4.3%
1964	3,734.0	5.8%	4.3%	2001	12,682.2	1.0%	3.7%
1965	3,976.7	6.5%	5.1%	2002	12,908.8	1.8%	3.2%
1966	4,238.9	6.6%	5.9%	2003	13,271.1	2.8%	2.9%
1967	4,355.2	2.7%	5.2%	2004	13,773.5	3.8%	2.7%
1968	4,569.0	4.9%	5.3%	2005	14,234.2	3.3%	2.5%
1969	4,712.5	3.1%	4.8%	2006	14,613.8	2.7%	2.9%
1970	4,722.0	0.2%	3.5%	2007	14,873.7	1.8%	2.9%
1971	4,877.6	3.3%	2.9%	2008	14,830.4	-0.3%	2.3%
1972	5,134.3	5.3%	3.4%	2009	14,418.7	-2.8%	0.9%
1973	5,424.1	5.6%	3.5%	2010	14,783.8	2.5%	0.8%
1974	5,396.0	-0.5%	2.8%	2011	15,020.6	1.6%	0.6%
1975	5,385.4	-0.2%	2.7%	2012	15,354.6	2.2%	0.7%
1976	5,675.4	5.4%	3.1%	2013	15,612.2	1.7%	1.1%
1977	5,937.0	4.6%	3.0%	2014	16,013.3	2.6%	2.1%
1978	6,267.2	5.6%	3.0%	2015	16,471.5	2.9%	2.2%
1979	6,466.2	3.2%	3.7%	2016	16,716.2	1.5%	2.2%
1980	6,450.4	-0.2%	3.7%				

38 | Appendix A: Statistical Appendix

The components of GDP also come from the U.S. Bureau of Economic Analysis.

Gross Domestic Product Expenditures in Nominal US Dollars in Millions

	Personal Consumption	Gross private domestic investment	Net exports	Government Consumption & Investment	Total		Personal Consumption	Gross private domestic investment	Net exports	Government Consumption & Investment	Total
1951	208,485	62,753	2,513	73,543	347,294	1984	2,498,155	820,093	-102,724	825,169	4,040,693
1952	219,471	57,267	1,164	89,826	367,728	1985	2,722,674	829,649	114,019	908,430	4,346,734
1953	233,012	60,415	-701	97,013	389,739	1986	2,898,411	849,144	-131,887	974,467	4,590,155
1954	239,924	58,068	404	92,750	391,146	1987	3,092,050	892,177	-144,770	1,030,760	4,870,217
1955	258,679	73,760	478	93,258	426,175	1988	3,346,889	938,964	-109,392	1,076,168	5,252,629
1956	271,569	77,682	2,361	98,518	450,130	1989	3,592,614	999,701	-86,741	1,151,919	5,657,693
1957	286,735	76,505	4,075	107,536	474,851	1990	3,825,630	993,453	-77,855	1,238,361	5,979,589
1958	296,027	70,949	538	114,531	482,045	1991	3,960,151	944,344	-28,615	1,296,163	6,174,043
1959	317,508	85,666	396	118,881	522,451	1992	4,215,654	1,013,014	-34,740	1,345,371	6,539,299
1960	331,578	86,477	4,204	121,024	543,283	1993	4,471,002	1,106,829	-65,174	1,366,061	6,878,718
1961	341,966	86,579	4,914	129,844	563,303	1994	4,741,016	1,256,483	-92,486	1,403,740	7,308,755
1962	363,108	96,976	4,100	140,931	605,115	1995	4,984,178	1,317,478	-89,758	1,452,162	7,664,060
1963	382,482	103,281	4,940	147,879	638,582	1996	5,268,071	1,432,057	-96,378	1,498,449	8,100,201
1964	411,193	112,153	6,914	155,526	685,786	1997	5,560,720	1,595,606	-101,970	1,554,159	8,608,515
1965	443,582	129,643	5,618	164,885	743,728	1998	5,903,033	1,735,330	-162,709	1,613,514	9,089,168
1966	480,597	144,186	3,864	186,392	815,039	1999	6,307,022	1,884,195	-256,631	1,726,038	9,660,624
1967	507,412	142,899	3,554	208,066	861,731	2000	6,792,396	2,033,750	-375,795	1,834,428	10,284,779
1968	557,449	156,922	1,351	226,758	942,480	2001	7,103,104	1,928,638	-368,683	1,958,765	10,621,824
1969	604,486	173,560	1,431	240,401	1,019,878	2002	7,384,053	1,924,988	426,464	2,094,937	10,977,514
1970	647,668	170,050	3,950	254,196	1,075,864	2003	7,765,529	2,027,947	503,655	2,220,849	11,510,670
1971	700,990	196,827	622	269,331	1,167,770	2004	8,260,018	2,276,678	-619,170	2,357,402	12,274,928
1972	769,431	228,145	-3,372	288,245	1,282,449	2005	8,794,112	2,527,109	-721,185	2,493,690	13,093,726
1973	851,143	266,930	4,111	306,365	1,428,549	2006	9,303,992	2,680,649	-770,947	2,642,194	13,855,888
1974	931,999	274,527	-814	343,113	1,548,825	2007	9,750,505	2,643,745	-718,542	2,801,927	14,477,635
1975	1,032,755	257,253	15,978	382,937	1,688,923	2008	10,013,648	2,424,810	723,067	3,003,191	14,718,582
1976	1,150,172	323,222	-1,631	405,824	1,877,587	2009	9,846,068	1,878,116	-395,436	3,089,091	14,418,739
1977	1,276,673	396,612	-23,093	435,759	2,085,951	2010	10,202,191	2,100,812	-512,657	3,174,026	14,964,372
1978	1,426,173	478,377	-25,368	477,387	2,356,571	2011	10,689,299	2,239,879	-570,995	3,168,743	15,517,926
1979	1,589,496	539,656	-22,546	525,537	2,632,143	2012	11,050,627	2,511,703	-565,662	3,158,586	16,155,254
1980	1,754,616	530,098	-13,056	590,847	2,862,505	2013	11,361,174	2,706,296	-492,005	3,116,051	16,591,516
1981	1,937,512	631,230	-12,520	654,734	3,210,956	2014	11,863,669	2,916,402	-509,509	3,157,046	17,427,608
1982	2,073,913	581,031	-19,974	710,021	3,344,991	2015	12,332,257	3,093,580	-524,042	3,218,919	18,120,714
1983	2,286,519	637,516	-51,642	765,744	3,638,137	2016	12,820,694	3,057,226	-521,239	3,267,795	18,624,476

Shares of Gross Domestic Product in Nominal US Dollars in Millions

	Personal Consumption	Private Investment	Net Exports	Govt.	Total		Personal Consumption	Private Investment	Net Exports	Govt.	Total
1951	60.0%	18.1%	0.7%	21.2%	100%	1984	61.8%	20.3%	-2.5%	20.4%	100%
1952	59.7%	15.6%	0.3%	24.4%	100%	1985	62.6%	19.1%	-2.6%	20.9%	100%
1953	59.8%	15.5%	-0.2%	24.9%	100%	1986	63.1%	18.5%	-2.9%	21.2%	100%
1954	61.3%	14.8%	0.1%	23.7%	100%	1987	63.5%	18.3%	-3.0%	21.2%	100%
1955	60.7%	17.3%	0.1%	21.9%	100%	1988	63.7%	17.8%	-2.1%	20.5%	100%
1956	60.3%	17.3%	0.5%	21.9%	100%	1989	63.5%	17.7%	-1.5%	20.4%	100%
1957	60.4%	16.1%	0.9%	22.6%	100%	1990	64.0%	16.6%	-1.3%	20.7%	100%
1958	61.4%	14.7%	0.1%	23.8%	100%	1991	64.1%	15.3%	-0.5%	21.0%	100%
1959	60.8%	16.4%	0.1%	22.8%	100%	1992	64.5%	15.5%	-0.5%	20.6%	100%
1960	61.0%	15.9%	0.8%	22.3%	100%	1993	65.0%	16.1%	-0.9%	19.9%	100%
1961	60.7%	15.4%	0.9%	23.1%	100%	1994	64.9%	17.2%	-1.3%	19.2%	100%
1962	60.0%	16.0%	0.7%	23.3%	100%	1995	65.0%	17.2%	-1.2%	18.9%	100%
1963	59.9%	16.2%	0.8%	23.2%	100%	1996	65.0%	17.7%	-1.2%	18.5%	100%
1964	60.0%	16.4%	1.0%	22.7%	100%	1997	64.6%	18.5%	-1.2%	18.1%	100%
1965	59.6%	17.4%	0.8%	22.2%	100%	1998	64.9%	19.1%	-1.8%	17.8%	100%
1966	59.0%	17.7%	0.5%	22.9%	100%	1999	65.3%	19.5%	-2.7%	17.9%	100%
1967	58.9%	16.6%	0.4%	24.1%	100%	2000	66.0%	19.8%	-3.7%	17.8%	100%
1968	59.1%	16.6%	0.1%	24.1%	100%	2001	66.9%	18.2%	-3.5%	18.4%	100%
1969	59.3%	17.0%	0.1%	23.6%	100%	2002	67.3%	17.5%	-3.9%	19.1%	100%
1970	60.2%	15.8%	0.4%	23.6%	100%	2003	67.5%	17.6%	-4.4%	19.3%	100%
1971	60.0%	16.9%	0.1%	23.1%	100%	2004	67.3%	18.5%	-5.0%	19.2%	100%
1972	60.0%	17.8%	-0.3%	22.5%	100%	2005	67.2%	19.3%	-5.5%	19.0%	100%
1973	59.6%	18.7%	0.3%	21.4%	100%	2006	67.1%	19.3%	-5.8%	19.1%	100%
1974	60.2%	17.7%	-0.1%	22.2%	100%	2007	67.3%	18.3%	-5.0%	19.4%	100%
1975	61.1%	15.2%	0.9%	22.7%	100%	2008	68.0%	16.5%	-4.9%	20.4%	100%
1976	61.3%	17.2%	-0.1%	21.6%	100%	2009	68.3%	13.0%	-2.7%	21.4%	100%
1977	61.2%	19.0%	-1.1%	20.9%	100%	2010	68.2%	14.0%	-3.4%	21.2%	100%
1978	60.5%	20.3%	-1.1%	20.3%	100%	2011	68.9%	14.4%	-3.7%	20.4%	100%
1979	60.4%	20.5%	-0.9%	20.0%	100%	2012	68.4%	15.5%	-3.5%	19.6%	100%
1980	61.3%	18.5%	-0.5%	20.6%	100%	2013	68.1%	16.2%	-2.9%	18.7%	100%
1981	60.3%	19.7%	-0.4%	20.4%	100%	2014	68.1%	16.7%	-2.9%	18.1%	100%
1982	62.0%	17.4%	-0.6%	21.2%	100%	2015	68.1%	17.1%	-2.9%	17.8%	100%
1983	62.8%	17.5%	-1.4%	21.0%	100%	2016	68.8%	16.4%	-2.8%	17.5%	100%

U.S. Gross Domestic Product Components

Average Component Shares

	1951 - 2016	1951 - 1969	1970 - 2016
Personal Consumption	63.2%	60.1%	64.4%
Gross Private Investment	17.2%	16.4%	17.6%
Net Exports	-1.4%	0.5%	-2.1%
Government	21.0%	23.1%	20.1%
Total	**100.0%**	**100.0%**	**100.0%**

Average Annual Growth Rates

	1951 - 2016	1951 - 1969	1970 - 2016
Personal Consumption	6.6%	6.2%	6.8%
Gross Private Investment	6.6%	6.5%	6.7%
Net Exports	-0.4%	60.5%	-25.0%
Government	6.7%	8.9%	5.8%
Total	**6.5%**	**6.7%**	**6.4%**

Inequality Metrics

The inequality metrics used in this eStudy are the following:

- Gini Coefficient
- Top 1% of Income
- Top 1% of Net Wealth

The Gini coefficient is an index that measures inequality and the computation of the Gini coefficient comes from U.S. Federal income tax returns. The Gini is based on the share of income in each stratum. The coefficient is between zero [where everyone earns the same] and one [where one person earns all the money]. **The formula is the following:**

Appendix A: Statistical Appendix

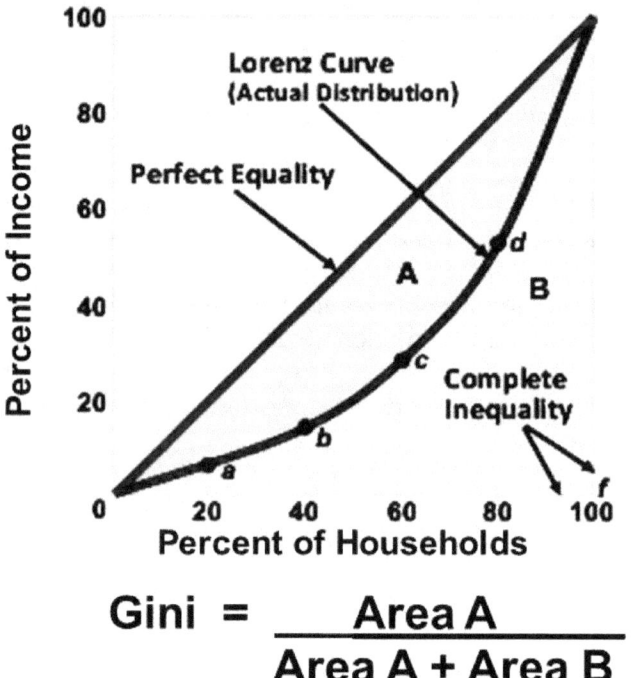

$$\text{Gini} = \frac{\text{Area A}}{\text{Area A} + \text{Area B}}$$

For this work, the Gini coefficient was not computed. Rather a series of data already computed was spliced together to get a continuous series that ran from 1944 to 2016. No splicing was needed for the Top 1% Income and Top 1% Net Wealth. All data comes from the

Chartbook that contains data for most countries of the world. The only data selected was that for the U.S. This file is located at www.chartbookofeconomicinequality.com.

Listed below are the Inequality Metrics and their 5-Year Moving Averages.

The Gini has been around since 1912 when Corrado Gini created it. The coefficient does not capture changes in the top 10% of income earners, let alone changes in the Top 1% of income earners. Likewise, the coefficient does not capture changes at the bottom where most of the poverty resides. While these shortcomings are important, the Gini is used in this eStudy because it is widely known, widely accepted and used by many institutions. In addition, the data are already compiled and available for a period spanning over 60 years.

Inequality Metrics - Annual Data

Year	Gini	Top 1% Income	Top 1% Net Wealth	Year	Gini	Top 1% Income	Top 1% Net Wealth
1944	0.379	10.5%	31.8%	1981	0.373	8.0%	23.3%
1945	0.358	11.1%	32.0%	1982	0.384	8.4%	23.7%
1946	0.366	11.8%	29.9%	1983	0.389	8.6%	22.7%
1947	0.374	11.0%	28.6%	1984	0.389	8.9%	22.9%
1948	0.369	11.3%	28.0%	1985	0.394	9.1%	23.1%
1949	0.372	10.9%	27.1%	1986	0.397	9.1%	22.9%
1950	0.375	11.4%	28.5%	1987	0.399	10.7%	24.6%
1951	0.362	10.5%	28.1%	1988	0.402	13.2%	26.5%
1952	0.362	9.8%	27.7%	1989	0.408	12.6%	26.6%
1953	0.368	9.1%	26.5%	1990	0.406	13.0%	26.7%
1954	0.373	9.4%	27.2%	1991	0.406	12.2%	26.0%
1955	0.365	9.2%	27.5%	1992	0.413	13.5%	27.6%
1956	0.361	9.1%	27.8%	1993	0.436	12.8%	27.7%
1957	0.364	9.0%	27.5%	1994	0.436	12.9%	27.6%
1958	0.362	8.8%	27.1%	1995	0.433	13.5%	27.9%
1959	0.367	8.7%	27.7%	1996	0.437	14.1%	28.6%
1960	0.368	8.4%	27.7%	1997	0.440	14.8%	29.5%
1961	0.376	8.3%	27.9%	1998	0.439	15.3%	30.7%
1962	0.366	8.3%	28.0%	1999	0.441	15.9%	31.5%
1963	0.364	8.2%	27.5%	2000	0.442	16.5%	32.3%
1964	0.365	8.0%	27.0%	2001	0.446	15.4%	31.3%
1965	0.363	8.1%	26.8%	2002	0.443	15.0%	30.2%
1966	0.359	8.4%	26.6%	2003	0.445	15.2%	30.3%
1967	0.362	8.4%	26.5%	2004	0.447	16.3%	31.5%
1968	0.351	8.4%	26.8%	2005	0.450	17.7%	32.1%
1969	0.353	8.0%	26.2%	2006	0.452	18.1%	32.8%
1970	0.357	7.8%	25.8%	2007	0.444	18.3%	34.0%
1971	0.359	7.8%	25.4%	2008	0.450	17.9%	36.1%
1972	0.362	7.8%	24.7%	2009	0.456	16.7%	36.1%
1973	0.360	7.7%	23.8%	2010	0.456	17.5%	37.6%
1974	0.354	8.1%	23.4%	2011	0.463	17.5%	37.4%
1975	0.359	8.0%	22.8%	2012	0.463	18.9%	38.8%
1976	0.359	7.9%	22.1%	2013	0.459	17.4%	37.0%
1977	0.362	7.9%	21.8%	2014	0.463	18.0%	37.2%
1978	0.363	8.0%	21.6%	2015	0.462	18.4%	
1979	0.366	8.0%	22.4%	2016	0.464		
1980	0.367	8.2%	22.5%				

Inequality Metrics for 5 Year Moving Average

	Gini	Top 1% Income	Top 1% Net Wealth		Gini	Top 1% Income	Top 1% Net Wealth
1944				1981	0.366	8.0%	22.3%
1945				1982	0.371	8.1%	22.7%
1946				1983	0.376	8.2%	22.9%
1947				1984	0.380	8.4%	23.0%
1948	0.369	11.1%	30.1%	1985	0.386	8.6%	23.1%
1949	0.368	11.2%	29.1%	1986	0.391	8.8%	23.0%
1950	0.371	11.3%	28.4%	1987	0.394	9.3%	23.2%
1951	0.371	11.0%	28.1%	1988	0.396	10.2%	24.0%
1952	0.368	10.8%	27.9%	1989	0.400	10.9%	24.7%
1953	0.368	10.3%	27.6%	1990	0.402	11.7%	25.4%
1954	0.368	10.0%	27.6%	1991	0.404	12.3%	26.1%
1955	0.366	9.6%	27.4%	1992	0.407	12.9%	26.7%
1956	0.366	9.3%	27.3%	1993	0.414	12.8%	26.9%
1957	0.366	9.1%	27.3%	1994	0.419	12.9%	27.1%
1958	0.365	9.1%	27.4%	1995	0.425	13.0%	27.4%
1959	0.364	9.0%	27.5%	1996	0.431	13.4%	27.9%
1960	0.364	8.8%	27.6%	1997	0.436	13.6%	28.3%
1961	0.367	8.7%	27.6%	1998	0.437	14.1%	28.9%
1962	0.368	8.5%	27.7%	1999	0.438	14.7%	29.6%
1963	0.368	8.4%	27.8%	2000	0.440	15.3%	30.5%
1964	0.368	8.2%	27.6%	2001	0.442	15.6%	31.1%
1965	0.367	8.2%	27.5%	2002	0.442	15.6%	31.2%
1966	0.363	8.2%	27.2%	2003	0.443	15.6%	31.1%
1967	0.363	8.2%	26.9%	2004	0.445	15.7%	31.1%
1968	0.360	8.2%	26.7%	2005	0.446	15.9%	31.1%
1969	0.358	8.2%	26.6%	2006	0.447	16.5%	31.4%
1970	0.356	8.2%	26.4%	2007	0.448	17.1%	32.1%
1971	0.356	8.1%	26.1%	2008	0.449	17.7%	33.3%
1972	0.356	7.9%	25.8%	2009	0.450	17.7%	34.2%
1973	0.358	7.8%	25.2%	2010	0.452	17.7%	35.3%
1974	0.358	7.8%	24.6%	2011	0.454	17.6%	36.2%
1975	0.359	7.9%	24.0%	2012	0.458	17.7%	37.2%
1976	0.359	7.9%	23.3%	2013	0.459	17.6%	37.4%
1977	0.359	7.9%	22.8%	2014	0.461	17.8%	37.6%
1978	0.359	8.0%	22.3%	2015	0.462	18.0%	
1979	0.362	8.0%	22.1%	2016	0.462		
1980	0.363	8.0%	22.1%				

Appendix A: Statistical Appendix

Inequality Metrics - Annual Rates of Change

	Gini	Top 1% Income	Top 1% Net Wealth		Gini	Top 1% Income	Top 1% Net Wealth
1944				1981	1.6%	-1.8%	3.7%
1945	-5.7%	5.1%	0.8%	1982	2.9%	4.5%	1.8%
1946	2.3%	6.2%	-6.8%	1983	1.3%	2.4%	-4.5%
1947	2.3%	-6.9%	-4.2%	1984	0.0%	3.4%	1.0%
1948	-1.4%	2.9%	-2.1%	1985	1.3%	2.3%	0.8%
1949	0.9%	-2.9%	-3.1%	1986	0.8%	0.4%	-0.7%
1950	0.7%	3.8%	4.9%	1987	0.5%	17.7%	7.4%
1951	-3.5%	-7.4%	-1.5%	1988	0.8%	22.5%	7.7%
1952	0.0%	-7.2%	-1.2%	1989	1.5%	-4.2%	0.3%
1953	1.6%	-6.9%	-4.4%	1990	-0.5%	2.9%	0.3%
1954	1.5%	3.4%	2.6%	1991	0.0%	-6.3%	-2.5%
1955	-2.1%	-2.2%	1.1%	1992	1.7%	10.8%	6.0%
1956	-1.2%	-1.0%	1.3%	1993	5.6%	-4.9%	0.4%
1957	0.7%	-1.2%	-1.3%	1994	0.0%	0.2%	-0.3%
1958	-0.5%	-1.7%	-1.5%	1995	-0.7%	5.3%	1.1%
1959	1.4%	-1.0%	2.4%	1996	0.9%	4.3%	2.4%
1960	0.2%	-4.5%	0.0%	1997	0.7%	4.7%	3.1%
1961	2.1%	-0.2%	0.7%	1998	-0.2%	3.5%	4.2%
1962	-2.5%	-0.8%	0.5%	1999	0.5%	3.8%	2.5%
1963	-0.7%	-1.3%	-1.8%	2000	0.2%	3.9%	2.6%
1964	0.2%	-1.8%	-1.8%	2001	0.9%	-6.8%	-3.0%
1965	-0.5%	0.6%	-0.9%	2002	-0.7%	-2.5%	-3.8%
1966	-1.0%	3.8%	-0.9%	2003	0.5%	1.5%	0.5%
1967	0.7%	0.7%	-0.3%	2004	0.4%	7.4%	3.8%
1968	-3.0%	-0.9%	1.2%	2005	0.7%	8.2%	2.0%
1969	0.6%	-4.0%	-2.4%	2006	0.4%	2.1%	2.3%
1970	1.1%	-2.7%	-1.3%	2007	-1.8%	1.5%	3.4%
1971	0.6%	-0.2%	-1.7%	2008	1.4%	-2.4%	6.3%
1972	0.8%	-0.4%	-2.7%	2009	1.3%	-6.8%	0.2%
1973	-0.6%	-0.2%	-3.5%	2010	0.0%	4.6%	3.9%
1974	-1.7%	4.9%	-1.9%	2011	1.5%	0.1%	-0.4%
1975	1.4%	-1.4%	-2.7%	2012	0.0%	8.1%	3.8%
1976	0.0%	-1.5%	-2.9%	2013	-0.9%	-7.7%	-4.7%
1977	0.8%	0.1%	-1.3%	2014	0.8%	3.2%	0.6%
1978	0.3%	0.7%	-1.0%	2015	-0.2%	2.3%	
1979	0.8%	1.0%	3.5%	2016	0.4%		
1980	0.3%	1.8%	0.6%				

Appendix B: Bibliography

9th Meeting of the Advisory Expert Group on National Accounts, "Distribution of Income, Consumption and Saving," Agenda Item 12.1, September 8-10, 2014 in Washington, DC.

Bloomberg Businessweek, "Piketty's Capital: An Economist's Inequality Ideas Are All the Rage", May 29, 2014.

Board of Governors of the Federal Reserve System, "Changes in U.S. Family Finances from 2010 to 2013: Evidence from the Survey of Consumer Finances," Federal Reserve Bulletin, September 2014, Vol. 100, No. 4.

Boston Consulting Group, "Global Wealth 2016, Navigating the New Client Landscape," June 2016.

Business Insider, "Chart of the Day: Rich People Really Love to Save Their Money," March 1, 2013.

Center for American Progress, "The Middle Class Squeeze," September 2014.

Center on Budget and Policy Priorities, "A Guide to Statistics on Historical Trends in Income Inequality," October 11, 2017.

Appendix B: Bibliography

Center on Budget and Policy Priorities, "Commentary: Ryan Report Distorts Safety Net's Picture," March 4, 2014.

Center on Budget and Policy Priorities, "JCT Estimates: Amended Senate Tax Bill Skewed to Top, Hurts Many Low- and Middle-Income Americans,' November 17, 2017.

Center on Budget and Policy Priorities, "Understanding Next Week's Census Figures on Poverty and Inequality," September 11, 2014.

Center on Budget and Policy Priorities, "What do OECD Data Really Show About U.S. Taxes and Reducing Inequality?" March 12, 2014.

Cingano, Federico, "Trends in Income Inequality and its Impact on Economic Growth," OECD Social, Employment and Migration Working Papers No. 163, 2014.

Cohen, Patricia, "What Could Raising Taxes on the 1% Do? Surprising Amounts," New York Times, October 16, 2015.

Conference of the GINI Project, "Income Inequality in Historical and Comparative Perspective," March 2010.

Credit Suisse Research Institute, "Global Wealth Report 2017", November 2017.

Appendix B: Bibliography | 49

Dalio, Ray, "Our Biggest Economic, Social and Political Issue The Two Economies: The Top 40% and the Bottom 60%, LinkedIn Blog, October 23, 2017 see https://www.linkedin.com/pulse/our-biggest-economic-social-political-issue-two-economies-ray-dalio/.

Economic Policy Institute, "Why America's Workers Need Faster Wage Growth – and What We Do About It." EPI Briefing Paper #382, August 27, 2014.

Finance and Development, "Why Inequality Throws Us Off Balance", 7 articles, September 2011, pages 6-29.

Fleming, Sam and Donnan, Shawn, "Middle Class Takes Financial Hit in Most U.S. Cities this Century," Financial Times, May 11, 2016.

Foglia, Antonio, "The Invention of Inequality," Project Syndicate, January 29, 2016.

Foroohar, Rana, "U.S. Inequality, The 'Haves and Have-Mores' in Digital America," Financial Times, August 7, 2017.

Furman, Jason, "Structural Challenges and Opportunities in the U.S. Economy," presentation to the London School of Economics on November 5, 2014.

Appendix B: Bibliography

Global Market Institue at Goldman Sachs, "Savings in America: Building Opportunities for All," Spring 2006.

Heise, Michael, "The Complexity of Inequality," Project Syndicate, December 9, 2016.

International Monetary Fund, "Inequality and Unsustainable Growth: Two Sides of the Same Coin," April 8, 2011, IMF Staff Discussion Paper SDN/11/08.

International Monetary Fund, "Income Inequality and Fiscal Policy," June 28, 2012, IMF Staff Discussion Paper SDN/12/08.

International Monetary Fund, "Fiscal Policy and Income Inequality," January 23, 2014, IMF Policy Paper.

International Monetary Fund, "Redistribution, Inequality and Growth," IMF Staff Discussion Paper, February 2014.

International Monetary Fund, "Income Polarization in the United States," IMF Working Paper W/16/12, June 2016.

International Monetary Fund Blog, "A New Twist in the Link Between Inequality and Economic Development," Francesco Grigoli, May 11, 2017, see https://blogs.imf.org/2017/05/11/a-new-twist-in-the-link-between-inequality-and-economic-development/.

International Monetary Fund, "Tackling Inequality," Fiscal Monitor, October 2017.

Journal of Economic Literature," Inequality and Economic Growth: The Perspective of the New Growth Theories," Volume 37, Number 4, December 1999, pages 1615-1660.

Journal of Political Economy, "Do the Rich Save More?" 2004, Volume 12, pages 397-444.

Journal of Post Keynesian Economics, "Savings and the Distribution of Income," Fall 1991, Volume 14, Number 1, pages 3-22.

Long, Heather, "Inequality in America Keeps Getting Uglier," CNN Money, December 22, 2016.

Lowrey, Annie, "Incomes Flat in Recovery, but Not for the 1%," New York Times, February 15, 2013.

Morgan Stanley, "Inequality and Consumption," September 22, 2014.

Moyo, Dambisa, "The Inequality Puzzle," Project Syndicate, February 18, 2016.

New York Times, "Liberty, Equality, Efficiency," March 9, 2014.

Organization for Economic Cooperation and Development, "An Overview of Growing Income

Inequalities in OECD Countries: Main Findings," 2011.

Organization for Economic Cooperation and Development, "Economic Outlook, Analysis & Forecast: The Equity Implications of Fiscal Consolidation," Economic Outlook Chapter 5, November 2012.

Organization for Economic Cooperation and Development, "Reducing Income Inequality While Boosting Economic Growth: Can It Be Done?" 2012.

Pew Research Center, "America's Shrinking Middle Class: A Close Look at Changes Within Metropolitan Areas," May 11, 2016.

Pew Research Center, "America's Wealth Gap Between Middle-Income and Upper-Income Families is Widest on Record," December, 17, 2014.

Pew Research Center, "Inequality, Joblessness are Top Threats in 2015, World Economic Forum Expects," November 7, 2014.

PEW Research Center, "Most See of Household Income and Federal Taxes, 2010," December 2013.

Qureshi, Zia, "Growing Out of Inequality," Project Syndicate, September 22, 2015.

Rodrik, Dani, "Good and Bad Inequality," Project Syndicate, December 11, 2014.

Rodrik, Dani, "How the Rich Rule," Project Syndicate, September 10, 2014.

Saez, Emmanuel, "Striking it Richer: The Evolution of Top Incomes in the United States (Updated with 2011 estimates), January 23, 2013.

Saez, Emmanuel, "Striking it Richer: The Evolution of Top Incomes in the United States (Updated with 2012 estimates), September 3, 2013.

Saez, Emmanuel and Zucman, Gabriel, "Wealth Inequality in the United States Since 1913: Evidence from Capitalized Income Tax Data," August 2015.

Spence, Michael, "Good and Bad Inequality," Project Syndicate, August 28, 2014.

Spence, Michael, "How Inequality Found a Political Voice," Project Syndicate, October 28, 2016.

Stiglitz, Joseph E., "Inequality and the American Child," Project Syndicate, December 11, 2014.

The Economist, "Inequality in America GINI in the Bottle," November 26, 2013.

The Pew Charitable Trusts, "The Precarious State of Family Balance Sheets, January 2015.

Appendix B: Bibliography

The World Bank, "Global Income Distribution From the Fall of the Berlin Wall to the Great Recession," Policy Research Working Paper 6719, December 2013.

The World Bank, "Economic Mobility and the Rise of the Latin American Middle Class", 2013.

Tyson, Laura, "The Rising Cost of U.S. Income Inequality," Project Syndicate, November 30, 2014.

U.S. Bureau of Economic Analysis, "Accounting for the Distribution of Income in the UN National Accounts", November 16, 2012.

U.S. Census Bureau, "Economic Inequality," July 2015.

U.S. Census Bureau, "Income and Poverty in the United States: 2013," Current Population Reports, September 2014.

U.S. Congressional Budget Office, "Trends in the Distribution of Household Income Between 1979 and 2007, October 2011.

U.S. Congressional Budget Office, "The Distribution of Household Income and Federal Taxes 2010," December 2013.

U.S. Congressional Budget Office, "The Distribution of Household Income and Federal Taxes 2011," November 2014.

Appendix B: Bibliography | 55

U.S. Congressional Budget Office, "The Distribution of Household Income and Federal Taxes 2013," June 2016.

U.S. Congressional Budget Office, "Trends in Family Wealth: 1989 to 2013," August 2016.

U.S. Congressional Budget Office and the Joint Committee on Taxation, "The Distribution of Asset Holdings and Capital Gains," August 2016.

U.S. Congressional Budget Office, "Trends in the Distribution of Household Income," presentation at the University of Michigan's 65th Annual Economic Outlook Conference, November 16, 2017.

U.S. Government Accountability Office, "Retirement Security, Most Households Approaching Retirement Have Low Savings," GAO-15-419, May 2015.

U.S. Joint Committee on Taxation, "Distribution Effects of the Chairman's Modification to the Chairman's Mark of the 'Tax Cuts and Jobs Act,' Scheduled for Markup by the Committee on Finance on November 15, 2017", November 17, 2017.

Washington Post, "Economic Mobility Hasn't Changed in a Half-century in America, Economists Declare," January 23, 2014.

Wolff, Edward N., "Inheritance and Inequality," Project Syndicate, October 21, 2014.

Appendix B: Bibliography

Acknowledgements

Special thanks to my Analytical Consultant Beth Jarosz who helped a great deal with the data, the analysis and reviewed an earlier draft. Thanks also go to Georges Sassine who reviewed an early draft and offered some great suggestions. Thanks also go to my Editor, Patricia Rice who improved the readability of this book.

www.ingramcontent.com/pod-product-compliance
Lightning Source LLC
Chambersburg PA
CBHW072235230526
45466CB00024B/1981